Sell Your Luxury Property For More Money

Greg Luther, Founder of Premier Luxury
Marketing Consultants

ISBN-10: 0692476253
ISBN-13: 978-0692476253

CONTENTS

WHY EVERY AFFLUENT HOMEOWNER SHOULD READ THIS BOOK

If you own a luxury property anywhere in America you'll quickly see that you need to read every page of this book immediately.

After being involved with over ten thousand real estate sales and purchases over the past decade, I've found that luxury homeowners are particularly at risk of losing their equity when it comes to the sale of their property. I'm talking about you. Let me explain…

You may be aware that in most states throughout the US, someone that works at a gas station can go to "real estate college" and become a fully licensed real estate agent in less than 3 weeks. They are then entrusted with the largest investment most people own and they are supposed to maximize the equity position of their clients with the newfound knowledge they've acquired.

This almost always ends in disaster. Worse, many homeowners in the luxury market have no idea how to choose the right representative for the sale of their home and it can many times cost them over $100,000 in equity

> **Choosing the wrong Real Estate Agent can cost you upwards of $100,000!**

(sometimes much more) once they do end up finally selling that asset. I have a few stories to share about that in the first few chapters here.

I've always found it disgusting that the people licensed by the state to handle such a tremendous financial asset are able to go through a few days of training and then be sent out into the world as a licensed agent to represent homeowners and home buyers on such a huge investment.

You now hold in your hands not only the instructions on how you can net more from the sale of your luxury level property but also some very specific "red flags" that you should avoid to ensure your home sale runs as smoothly as possible.

I've structured this book to put you the homeowner in control of maximizing the equity in your home.

Simply put, with the knowledge you have in your hands here, you can sell your home and even buy your next home with a little known secret that only the top real estate professionals in America are even familiar with.

It's a secret of the wealthy and now you have the ability to peek behind the curtain to see how your family can sell your home for more money while avoiding the common catastrophe we see so often in the more affluent real estate price ranges.

It seems like every year that goes by, we affluent citizens of America have a larger target on our back financially. Everyone from Uncle Sam to the politicians to the local news stations want to take away our security (spelled M-O-N-E-Y) and make us out to be evil in some kind of way.

After all, they think the top 1% is evil anyway. This is a popular belief by the rest of the world as it makes them feel better about their own lack of success. But most importantly, it puts the affluent households directly on the front lines of the firing squad when it comes to preserving our wealth.

One of the best signs of wealth can be the property that you live in and unfortunately for many homeowners, they make mistakes in choosing an agent to represent their best interests and ensure that you net as much as possible from the sale of that estate.

I'll be telling you about what to do and more importantly what not to do as you consider putting your home on the market and selling it for as much as possible. But let me warn you not to do ANYTHING until you've read this book.

This will arm you with the knowledge to make all of the right moves and represent your own best interest when staging the home, choosing a marketing consultant, negotiating the best sales price and even the detailed terms that can weigh things heavily in your favor.

I've personally spoken to, coached and mentored over 30,000 real estate agents all over the country. I've witnessed some huge wins and huge losses when it comes to the marketing and sale of an exclusive luxury priced estate like your own.

You'll read about some of those stories in this book. You'll see where families unknowingly made a drastic error in the sale of their home and cost themselves well over $100,000.

On the flip side of that coin though, you'll see how smart homeowners in the affluent markets are taking advantage of a little known secret that the one percenters utilize on a regular basis.

But most importantly for you, I'll be exposing the cold hard truth about real estate agents and the marketing of properties like yours that I can assure you has never been disclosed before today.

And frankly, you'll be shocked! I can assure you that this will be a tremendous learning lesson for you and once you learn how targeted these marketing and exposure techniques are, you'll be extremely excited at the thought of how this will work on your home.

With the thousands of luxury home sales we've been

involved with all over the country, it's not uncommon for the property owners we work with to ask about utilizing this type of marketing and exposure in their own line of work.

Obviously with several of these luxury level properties, the people selling them oftentimes own their own small business. Several have utilized some of the secrets in this book to not only sell their house for more money, but also to increase the results in their own business. After all, extensive target marketing can be duplicated in all lines of work.

You'll want to pay close attention to several details in this book. When you read about homeowners that have lost over $500,000 from the sale of their luxury property, you should learn from their mistakes.

When you read about families that earned an additional $300,000 more than anyone thought they'd ever get, that will be sage advice for you as well.

In all cases good or bad, it was their own fault. And in the following pages, you'll learn how to protect your money, maximize the sale of your property and do it all in a confident manner as you've prepared yourself prior to starting the process.

You are well aware that the two most valuable things when going into a large transaction is **knowledge** and **confidence**. You'll have both today.

Since you are one of our nation's Most Valuable Players, I know that your time is extremely important. I can assure you that what you'll read in the coming pages will be worth your time and bluntly speaking, it can put hundreds of thousands of additional dollars in your pocket by utilizing some of the secrets shared in the coming chapters.

Before you get started, I'll go ahead and give you a resource that will be of massive value to you when selling your home. It will be extremely helpful for you and just might put a lot more money in your pocket so you may want to stop and check it out immediately.

Go to **www.PremierLuxuryMarketing.com** and learn how you can sell your property for more than you ever thought possible.

So buckle up and get ready. You are about to learn the secrets that lots of wealthy people are using to create major wins for themselves while also avoiding the common pitfalls when selling their home.

CHAPTER 1

Why Selling Your Luxury Home In Today's Market Is Different

Just about one decade ago, getting the most amount of money from the sale of your home was easy. You could just call the "area specialist" real estate agent and know that they'd have the contacts to get the home sold for your asking price.

Heck, most of the time the seller could even price their home a little bit above what they thought it was worth and may still get an offer.

If you take that approach in today's market, you'll likely end up unsold, price reduced, stressed out of your mind and arguing with your spouse because you can't get the home sold.

And in the coming pages you'll learn that in most areas of the United States, this is happening on more than 50% of all home sales.

It's a shocking fact but also a sobering reality for luxury homeowners that want to sell their home for the most amount of money.

Why Is It So Hard?

Marketing is more important in today's fast paced society than ever before. There is a constant barrage of companies trying to get your attention and we try to mentally block out most of their attempts.

The latest stat I've seen shows that in America, we are exposed to over 5,100 ads per day for various products and services.

CBS News did this study and they found that in the late 70's we saw less than 500 ads per day. Today there are so many that people don't even pay attention. More than 10 times the number of ads we viewed just a few decades ago, yet we are blind to most of their attempts at capturing our attention.

This isn't a problem for you when you are the

consumer but if you are trying to sell something (especially a luxury priced home) you'd better know how to get the attention of the absolutely best quality buyer that would pay you the most amount of money under terms acceptable to you.

Marketing Just Doesn't Work Like It Used To

Marketing doesn't work like it used to. That creates a problem in that if you have a unique product (or in your case, a very unique house) it's nearly impossible to get the home exposed to the most opportune buyers, each of which would be willing to pay you at or above your asking price to get the home.

However on the other side of that coin, if you figure out this hidden secret to massive exposure, you can potentially sell your property for $100,000 to $300,000 more than you ever thought possible.

The world called "advertising" has changed drastically over the past few years and frankly, there's a lot of hype out there that can be chalked up to nothing more than a load of BS.

I'm sure you've heard of all the latest and greatest ways of promoting houses, cars, businesses and more. Most of it is a load of crap and it's nothing more than a cheap alternative to something that actually creates real results.

I don't have to tell you that "cheap" usually costs you more than it saves you. This is true with everything in life. And when it comes to the sale of a million dollar plus house, it can cost you more money than you'd ever imagine.

I'll share a story or two with you about that shortly.

Since I'm involved with the inner workings of thousands of property sales all over the country, I feel I owe it to you to give you a few damaging admissions.

As a matter of fact, you should know the bare naked truth about the sale of real estate and specifically within the Luxury Market, some of the biggest secrets that the so called "luxury specialists" hope you never hear about.

You'll learn about these facts in this book and most importantly, I'll show you how you can sell your property faster, for a lot more money than you ever imagined.

Selling Your Home Is MUCH Different

Selling your home in today's market is MUCH different than before and a Targeted Marketing Approach is absolutely crucial to your overall success.

You already know that price is a function of supply and demand so the more demand that can be created on your home, the higher the final sales price will be. As the saying goes, "this isn't the old market" and the specific Targeted Marketing Approach used for your property can make the difference of $100,000 or even $300,000 in some cases.

You are undoubtedly aware that there's a big difference between the average, median priced home and the exclusive luxury market throughout your city.

Very small details in a luxury home sale can make the difference of failure or success when it comes to selling the property at all, let alone for the price you'd like to get.

The way the home is staged, the way it is marketed and the way you target a specific type of affluent home buyer is extremely costly, but in many cases it nets you ten times that marketing investment in the form of a much faster selling time and a higher selling price.

If you look around your neighborhood, you'll see that there are a few homes that have been sitting on the market for months and months on end.

Of course they thought their home would sell very quickly (all homeowners believe this) and they just knew that it was worth every penny that they were asking.

They made a critical mistake and later, the homeowner is then forced to reduce their price in an effort to sell their "stale" home and oftentimes it doesn't sell at all.

It happens in every affluent neighborhood in America and for the first time ever revealed to the public, in the coming chapters you'll learn why that is and how you can avoid it happening to you.

Oh by the way…

Who I am and why you should listen to me…

My name is Greg Luther and I've been involved in real estate for nearly two decades now. I teach sales and marketing techniques to real estate agents all over the country and have over 30,000 agents involved with our trainings at one level or another.

I'm also the founder of Premier Luxury Marketing Consultants which is a group of the most well trained, target marketing Luxury Real Estate agents in all of the United States. Each of these agents has gone through an extensive luxury marketing training and they are involved with continuous training to learn from each other in a mastermind setting of the most brilliant minds in the real estate world.

You can find out more about this Luxury Designation and even see if we have certified agents in your area by going to www.PremierLuxuryMarketing.com

In the meantime, let's get back to what it's going to take for you to net a much higher sales price when you go to sell your home.

And a quick question for you here. If I could show you how to net an additional $50,000 or $100,000 from the sale of your home, would I have your attention? Then flip the page and let me tell you exactly how to do that. First, I need to disclose the "big myth" in real estate that you need to be aware of.

CHAPTER 2

The Biggest Myth In Luxury Real Estate Which Can Cost You Hundreds of Thousands of Dollars

So this is a damaging admission. As someone involved in real estate sales every day, it pains me to admit it but this is information that you as an affluent homeowner need to know.

I questioned myself as to if I should disclose this information or not but if you truly want to net as much as possible from your home sale, you need to know about the "dirty little secret" in real estate.

The "Dirty Little Secret" in Real Estate

It's totally against everything I should be disclosing and with me working with upwards of 30,000 real estate agents around the country, a handful of them will be upset that I'd publicly disclose this dirty little secret in a public fashion like this.

The truth is that most real estate agents are grossly overpaid.

I know, that may not be much of a surprise to you but if you are going to be selling your home, especially in the luxury market, there are some very important facts that you need to know.

The job called "real estate agent" has essentially became commoditized due to the advancements in technology.

Everything for Only $500?

So the things that traditional real estate agents do can actually be done for less than $500. So listing it on the MLS, putting a sign in the yard, doing an open house, having it on 114 websites, etc. can all be done for a flat fee of far less than $500 even in your town.

But the fact is, it will nearly NEVER sell your property. As a matter of fact, you actually have a much more likely outcome of stigmatizing your own property, causing it to go stale on the market and causing the general public to believe that the home isn't worth your asking price.

This is the last thing you'd ever want to do and I'm more than happy to show you a better way.

Why The Johnson's $1,500,000 Home Hadn't Sold

As a quick story for reference, I'll tell you about a homeowner that was selling their home for $1,500,000. To be discreet here, let's call them the Johnson Family.

Like most homeowners in the affluent market, the Johnson's interviewed a couple of real estate agents and of course they had complete confidence that their home would sell regardless of who handled the listing because the home was so desirable in their own mind.

It had lots of amenities and was pretty much a "one of a kind" luxury home.

In turn, they chose the real estate agent that sends out lots of postcards and various marketing pieces in their neighborhood which made them assume that this agent is the "area specialist".

They figured since they see her name and face all the time, she's probably the best one for the job. That only makes sense right?

The agent came in and gave an impressive presentation. She also showed that she just sold a neighbor's house just a couple of streets over. This was all that The Johnson's needed to make a decision so they listed with her right there on the spot.

They had confidence in the agent simply because they recognized her from previous marketing pieces they'd received over the past year and they made a decision based on this one fact alone.

They listed it with her for $1,500,000 and felt pretty good about the commission they agreed to as well.

Since they had supreme confidence in their home and their agent, they assumed this would be an extremely fast process.

Things started out well, there were several showings and the communication was great for the first two weeks.

After that, it started to feel like their home sale was no longer important as the agent was more focused on attracting even more sellers, rather than selling the one's she had.

They were still getting lots of postcards and marketing pieces that were being distributed in the area that had nothing more than the agent's face and name promoted all over it just like the dozens of other pieces they'd received in the past.

Fast forward 6 months and the only time The Johnson's heard from their agent was when she was trying to get a price reduction

"The market has shown that we can't sell for $1,500,000"

because in her own words *"the market has shown that we can't sell for $1,500,000"*.

6 Months Later....

So here they sit, 6 months later with a reduced asking price of $1,400,000 and the home still hasn't sold. Worse, the showings are incredibly sporadic and the agent is rarely returning their phone calls when they have questions.

In turn, the home that they know is in perfect condition and highly desirable with dozens of amenities hasn't sold at all.

They are $100,000 lower than they thought they'd be, and the neighborhood specialist has failed. They then realized that they are stuck in a long term agreement with no end in sight and as each passing month ticked by, things were looking more and more like a complete bust.

On a whim, Mrs. Johnson decided to get online and see

if she can find out reasons that her home may not have sold. It simply didn't make sense that they have such a desirable home, they always get compliments from guests and they feel as though $1,500,000 is truly what their home was worth.

They've been sitting for months at a reduced price of $1,400,000 and still no measurable results. She starts looking at the marketing of luxury priced homes and stumbles across one of the big nationally recognized sites in www.PremierLuxuryMarketing.com

She gets in contact with a local agent that is certified as a Premier Luxury Marketing Consultant and though they certainly don't want to go through the nightmare of listing their home again, they'd like to get this agent's opinion as to why in the world their gorgeous home hasn't sold.

What they found out was nothing short of shocking...

First and foremost, they found out the real details behind the "area specialist" that had their home listed. Yes, she'd listed seven homes in the past six months within that neighborhood. And two of them sold.

Yes you read that right. She'd listed 7 and sold only 2. As it turns out, they thought she was the most qualified agent because she knows the area and seems to be working lots of homes in the community yet they later found out that the agent failed 5 out of 7 times.

Arguably, she is actually reducing the value of every single home in the neighborhood due to the downward pressure she is creating on price with each of her listings.

As each of those homes reduce their price on the open market, that in turn creates lower values for virtually every owner in the community.

Truth be told, she was really good at promoting herself, but horrible at marketing houses. The Johnson Family was unfortunately on the receiving end of someone that does a lot of self-promotion but little to no house-promotion.

They Finally Sold for 99.7% of Their Asking Price!

You'll be happy to know that they were able to secure that Premier Luxury Marketing Consultant after their previous listing agreement expired and their property sold in 41 days for 99.7% of their asking price.

They quickly realized that they needed someone that understood how to do Direct Target Marketing to the most opportune buyer rather than working with an agent that had lots of ads bragging about how many listings she had in the area.

They learned a lot of inside secrets including the reasons you can't sell a luxury property by just listing it on the MLS and waiting for something to happen.

The Biggest Myth...

You see the biggest myth in luxury real estate is that you should go with someone that appears to do a lot of business in the area.

We've often called this the "kiss of death" for luxury homeowners all over the country and it happens all the time. It's statistically one of the biggest mistakes a homeowner says they've made when their home hasn't sold.

In interviewing a handful of them, we found that hindsight being 20/20, they realized that the only reason they agreed to hire that agent in the first place was simply that it was someone they recognized or that had listed a high percentage of homes.

Just remember that in most situations, your perception isn't the true reality. Let me explain...

Who Should You Hire?

In truth, you need to choose someone that has the credentials, knowledge and credibility to sell your property to the most opportune prospects by investing their own money in a significant marketing campaign.

Many times in the luxury market, the home will sell to an off-market buyer rather than a buyer that is actively looking for a property. Since this is the case, it's important to go with an agent that understands direct marketing.

Truth be told, regardless how many magazine ads an agent runs, virtual tours they create or drones they fly in the air to take photos and videos of your house, it's not going to sell if advertised where traditional buyers are shopping.

That means the MLS, the brochures, the magazines and the newspapers are NOT getting to the best buyers that would fall in love with your property and pay a premium price for it.

> **The best buyers DO NOT come from MLS listings or newspaper and magazine ads.**

I'll explain in more detail shortly so that you have a complete grasp on what it takes to truly net more profit from the sale of your home.

Being that you are affluent yourself, you obviously know that the only thing more important than having the right instruction on what to do is simply understanding what NOT to do so you can avoid financial disaster.

I could give a laundry list 20 pages long on things not

to do but let's first talk about how you can sell your home for more money based on the amenities it has to offer to prospective buyers.

CHAPTER 3

How To Get A Higher Sales Price From Your Premium Amenities

So now you understand that a Luxury Marketing Consultant is the best option when selling your property if you truly want to net the highest price possible. But let's discuss the reason this is so true, specifically for your home and in your town.

Undoubtedly, you originally purchased your home as somewhat of a "trophy home". In America, the home we live in is a sign of well-deserved success.

Generally speaking, the affluent homeowners truly deserve the lavish lifestyle as they've contributed the most to society, thus allowing for the biggest rewards.

Thinking back to when you first laid eyes on your house, you certainly fell in love with specific amenities of the property itself.

What Made YOU Fall In Love With Your Home?

It may have been the location, the neighborhood, what the lot backs up to or specific features on the interior like a home theatre, a home office, a wine cellar or a gourmet kitchen that creates the "wow" effect when you have guests over.

All of these factors created an internal urge for you to want this property over anything else that was on the market at that time.

The home was a great match for YOUR specific wants and needs. That doesn't mean it's right for everyone, but it was absolutely perfect for you, thus the reason you bought it or had it built.

The key to successful real estate sales

The key to successful real estate sales is to find a perfect match between house and buyer. If we know which amenities are available in the home, we can create a marketing campaign geared towards the people that would be a perfect fit for that type of property.

This is a much more detailed process in today's world than it's ever been before. Each individual amenity would be a big turn on for some and a turn off for others.

If I'm a boater, I'd love to buy a house on the water. However, if that's not something that excites me, I wouldn't want to pay a premium for an amenity that I wouldn't enjoy on a regular basis.

A targeted marketing approach can put your home in front of the best buyers as it will simply use particular interests or "selects" to identify the best candidates regardless if they are in the market right now or not.

> **A Target Marketing approach can put your home in front of the BEST buyers**

Let's look at what we are referring to here.

So you are likely aware that a highly successful marketing firm can buy a list of all subscribers to Wine Connoisseur Magazine.

If they cross reference (merge-purge) that list with those that also have an annual household income of $600,000 it may be a good list of buyers for your luxury home that has a large walk-in wine cellar.

In a more simplistic explanation, someone that has a high net worth and an affinity for wine would want your house more than someone that doesn't drink alcohol at all.

By getting a targeted list of those that do, they'd be the ones willing to consider a purchase of the property if presented in the right way.

Each of your home amenities can be marketed to a specific group of potential buyers that may be willing to not only buy it, but also pay a premium. Let's look at a really good example here.

Imagine your home is on the water and has a large dock and boat lift. A premier marketer may decide to acquire a list of all people that have a boat registered in their name in your state, that currently live in a home worth between $500,000 and $800,000 and is located within 30 miles of you, they've lived there for at least five years, have at least two teenage children in the home, subscribe to Entrepreneur Magazine, own stocks, like to travel and have a credit score of over 720.

Did you know that this list is available?

And thousands of others with the same type of list selects?

THIS is how you sell a property for a significant

premium.

It's how you find buyers that would have a rabid response to a home just like yours.

If You Can Describe Them ...
We Can Find Them

The exciting part is that as much as you can describe the perfect buyer for your house, a professional marketer can get a list that resembles that description!

The downside is that less than 1% of all real estate agents in America even know how to acquire a list like this, let alone market your property to them correctly.

That's why it's so important that you work with an agent that is certified as a Premier Luxury Marketing Consultant.

Your home is worth a great deal of money due to the SPECIFIC amenities it offers. But those are only worth a large sum of money to the type of buyer that will appreciate it just as you do.

Let me give you an example. Myself, I own over 40 racehorses that race all over the country. We breed them, raise them and race them.

As a side note, be sure you never invest in anything that

eats while you sleep! Anyway, if your home has an 8 car garage, the agent would be wasting their time marketing that home to me as it doesn't fit my needs.

We have 2 cars and one boat. Anything more than that is a waste of money and space as far as a home that I'd purchase.

If you were asking $2,000,000 for your home I wouldn't have an interest. As a matter of fact, if you knocked off a half-million dollars it still doesn't fit my needs here.

Can you see where we are going with this?

Now on the contrary, if your house has a 3 or 4 car garage but also has a huge horse barn and acreage, I'd be highly interested.

Understand that I'm not really even in the market to buy a house right now but if I found a place that I could have everything in one spot and I could keep an eye on it, I'd respond immediately.

Acreage and a barn and a nice house?

I'm interested!

This would keep me from paying to store my boat somewhere and it would eliminate the $40,000 plus I'm spending every single month for training and boarding of my horses in various parts of the United States.

I'd pay a premium and would immediately consider a move.

Again, I'm not even shopping for a home but in the luxury market, off-market buyers will pay more.

They aren't even necessarily looking for a home but when presented with something that they have an interest in, they'll immediately consider a purchase regardless of it being perceived as an "under market" home.

They'll pay at or above market value. They would make the move and would pay you a premium for the home that best fits their needs, even if they weren't shopping around in magazines, looking at homes or working under some strict deadline to buy.

They could simply stumble across your home (in their mailbox) and make the decision to check it out.

Keep in mind that subscribers to horse magazines, clubs, associations and various groups or memberships are all readily available to a professional marketer.

They can then merge-purge (or cross reference) that list with those that also own X number of horses, have an annual household income of X and a credit score of X while also owning a home within 30 miles of this subject property's location.

These lists can vary from time to time. Sometimes we can get all of the info and sometimes we only get some of it. But using this information gives your home a HUGE leg-up in attracting a highly qualified, highly motivated buyer.

And the more targeted we are, the higher the likelihood that you'll get someone willing to pay a premium.

This is who your home needs to be marketed to. It's the group of buyers that would pay a premium for your property and they are not shopping the competing homes that are for sale in your town.

It certainly beats running ads in a bunch of glossy magazines and on 114 websites wouldn't you say?

The examples I've given you here are very basic. A licensed agent that is fully trained in these superior marketing techniques will know which of your amenities would be the most marketable.

Tennis court? There's a great list available for people with that interest.

Home office? We can get a hyperactive response from those that run a home business and earn over $1,000,000 per year.

Gourmet kitchen? Yes, there's a great list select we can use for that too.

Helicopter pad?

Outbuildings?

Acreage?

Mother-in-Law suite?

In home theatre?

All of these amenities and thousands more can be marketed to the absolute most qualified and opportune buyers if you get a marketing consultant that is willing to invest in some highly specific targeted lists.

This is a far superior approach compared to what a traditional agent will do. You are probably familiar with their routine. They list it on the MLS, have a photographer come out, run some magazine ads and create glossy brochures, then go right back to marketing their agent photo and telling everyone how famous they are.

Let's be honest here. They are good at promoting themselves, not their properties. They are good at talking about how big their brokerage is or that it's recognized as a "luxury home brokerage" yet they won't reveal the biggest dirty secret of all… But I will…

Generally in the luxury market you'll find that on average, less than 50% of their homes even sell at all, let alone at the price they originally promised.

In researching the most up to date information prior to the publication of this book, I found that when looking at the top three agents in 10 different major markets (30 agents total), virtually 100% of those 30 agents routinely get $100,000 and $200,000 price reductions on their listings over and over for a period of a full one year listing agreement!

In turn, obviously this means they've over promised and under delivered just to begin beating up the asking price later when they get no results.

Meanwhile, there's a significant chance that they've never invested in even one marketing list to promote the property to the absolutely perfect candidates. They've just added a little square for your home underneath that big picture of their smiling face with a phone stuck in their ear.

I don't have to tell you that $100,000 reduction, even on a one or two million dollar home is a huge cut. And worse, it comes directly from your equity. But there's a better approach. With the knowledge you are acquiring now, it's likely the approach you'll choose so that you can avoid the common pitfalls these agents fell into.

Who Is Going To
Buy Your Home?

Let's think about the type of buyer that's going to buy a luxury home like yours.

Do you think they are going to pick up a real estate magazine from the take-out Chinese restaurant?

Grab one leaving the local grocery store?

In reality, the typical real estate agent's marketing generally does nothing to attract clients and the only people that actually view the home in person are those working with other agents that found the property in the MLS.

It would only make sense that if someone actually called from the marketing they would reach the listing agent right? And the listing agent would show it? If you've sold a luxury home in the past using a commodity agent, you've seen that it rarely happens that way and the home is rarely (if ever) marketed correctly.

In turn, their marketing does absolutely nothing to promote your home and truly only promotes the agent, the brokerage and their services. After all, who exactly are they trying to target and why would they think that this type of egotistical marketing would get an affluent buyer to buy a particular home?

When thinking about the specific benefits of your property, you want to decide on the best features of the home that will likely get a buyer extremely excited about your home in lieu of anything else that's out there on the market today.

What makes your home unique?

If those features are marketed correctly and you find an agent that truly understands target marketing, you'll likely sell your home for a much higher price and won't need to negotiate at all because the buyer will see your home as one of a kind.

I've trained several agents around the country on this type of target marketing and they've experienced the massive success it creates. It's tremendously beneficial for the home sellers that they represent. To see if there are any certified Premier Luxury Marketing Consultants in your area, go to: **PremierLuxuryMarketing.com**

In the meantime, you'll want to start thinking about a long list of things that make your home unique, special and valuable. Marketed to the right type of buyer, you can net a much higher price from the sale of your home.

There's a good chance that this book was referred to

you by a PLMC certified real estate agent. Check out the website to ensure that they are in fact certified, then schedule a meeting to discuss some of the best ways to expose your property to the most opportune buyers.

.

CHAPTER 4

When Is The Best Time To Sell?

Should you sell in the Summer time? The Winter time? Maybe wait a year or two? Is now the right time? The answer can be more complicated than you might assume.

Most homeowners in the more affluent market realize that delaying their goals is in effect delaying their desired outcome. That alone can be a huge price to pay. Looking at it from that perspective, the best time to sell is immediately.

There's no sense in holding up your family's goals in an effort to "time the market".

There are a lot of so called professionals out there that will tell you now is a great time to sell. All you have to do is change the channel and the people on that channel will tell you it's a horrible time to sell! Everyone wants to predict the market and exactly 50% of them are wrong every time.

Certainly in the luxury real estate world, consumer confidence can have a lot to do with the public's willingness to invest in a high priced home.

When the wealthy start to feel confident (and safe) with what's going on nationally and even internationally, they are more liberal with their money. They'll buy bigger cars, bigger houses, 2nd and 3rd residences and much more.

In other times, they choose to play it safe.

Sometimes even when they have the ability to purchase, they'll be more reserved.

However, experience shows us that regardless of the price range your home is in, "playing it safe" is a different figure for different people.

As an example, the people that can afford $8 million may only buy for $4 million.

The people that can afford $4 million may only buy for $2 million.

And the people that can easily buy themselves a $2 million dollar home may be more comfortable at $1 million.

There Is No "Bad" Time To Sell

So there's truly no "bad" time to sell and it makes the most sense to make the move whenever it fits best for your family's needs.

If you are selling when the market is a little bit lower, the home you are buying will also be a little lower.

When you are selling at the peak, the home you are moving to is also at the peak. Essentially it all levels out.

The big advantage for all of the homeowners and agents I've been involved with is that with a superior marketing plan, we can always find someone that's willing to pay a premium price for the perfect home.

Good markets and bad markets, crazy dot-com markets and even recessions, we've moved lots of million dollar and multi-million dollar homes.

The key is simply targeting that most opportune buyer with a very specific direct marketing approach. This can mean the difference of tens of thousands of dollars and sometimes more.

In reality, the best time to sell your luxury priced

property is when it best fits your family's needs and plans.

Most importantly, you want to ensure you don't delay those plans because of the market or some misconstrued financial reason.

There will always be ups and downs in the economy and the real estate market in general. There will always be buyers too.

Regardless if it's a red hot market or the depths of a recession, homes are selling, particularly if they are marketed correctly.

Far too many homeowners make the mistake of "guessing" on their timing of the market and it generally hurts them in more ways than you could ever imagine.

They put off their goals, they delay their move for 6 months, a year and sometimes even longer.

> **Don't put off your goals or delay your move waiting for a "perfect" market.**

Cardinal mistake I've seen far too often over the past couple of decades and it usually comes back to bite them in the butt.

Particularly if you are buying another house after your upcoming home sale, you'll be buying in the same market as you are selling in so it all averages out.

The Luxury Market is Least Affected By Market Fluctuations

As you know, the affluent are the least affected by market fluctuations so we've found that small dips in the real estate market will hurt the median price ranges in any given marketplace much more than it will cause an adjustment in the luxury price ranges.

Luxury buyers and sellers aren't adversely affected by small bubbles and minimal economic changes.

We've found that the affluent and ultra-affluent households in America rarely have financial issues as they are usually very wise and they make good decisions.

In turn, during hot markets, they will make decisions based on emotion and back it up with logic, then during tougher economies, they'll make decisions based on logic, backed up with emotion.

Read that paragraph again…

Basically, they'll be more frivolous with their spending during hot markets but will still make large purchases in slower markets as long as it's something they truly want for their family.

In turn, packaging up the product being sold to them is crucially important regardless of the type of market you are experiencing at any time.

Sure, any old agent can put your home on the MLS and wait on a purchase contract to come along but to maximize your sale price, you have to take a MUCH different approach.

Creating an Emotional Connection = Higher Sale Price

Our goal is to find someone that will make a buying decision on your home based on emotion. If we can get them emotionally tied to your property because it fits their hobbies, interests or specific business or personal needs, you'll get a premium price.

There's no profit to be had when going with an agent that will list your home, then continue marketing their face and their service.

When it's time for your family to sell the home, you need an agent that understands a target marketing approach and will spend a great deal of time and their own money to promote the property to the best group of high quality, highly qualified buyers. This can net you a much higher price from the sale of the home.

Finding someone like this up until a couple of years ago was nearly impossible. That's where I saw a tremendous need that was desired by luxury homeowners all over the country and it's the reason I decided to fix that problem with the Premier Luxury Marketing Consultants program.

CHAPTER 5

Attracting Affluent Buyers That Will Pay Top Dollar For Your House

When thinking about how you can net the most amount of money from the sale of your home, it's important to first understand the difference between the affluent and the ultra-affluent buyer.

You can then determine which would be the best buyer for the property. There's a monstrous difference between affluent and ultra-affluent. Additionally, they both respond to different types of offers. Let's look at the difference here.

This definition will vary greatly depending on what industry you are in. As an example, many stock brokers believe a client worth over $10,000,000 is affluent and those worth over $75,000,000 are ultra-affluent.

Who Qualifies As An Affluent Buyer?

In the real estate world, and for luxury marketing purposes, we generally classify anyone with a net worth of more than $2,000,000 as an affluent buyer whereas those with a net worth of over $7,000,000 are considered ultra-affluent.

Of course depending on their financial ability, some will pay all cash for a house while others will have the ability to qualify for a mortgage well into the millions. Either way, they may be a good candidate as a buyer for your home provided you are attracting the RIGHT type of prospect.

I'll give you an example. Most people would be very excited to get a call from Gatorade where they are asking you to star in a television commercial for them. If they offered you $500,000 for 60 seconds worth of footage, that's even better right?

However if you are LeBron James or Michael Jordan, you'd likely not only be disinterested, but would laugh at the company because that isn't a lot of money to someone of the ultra-affluent caliber in the sports world. It takes a lot more to get the ultra-affluent excited.

The same is true in real estate. A property worth $400,000 to $800,000 in some markets is considered a "trophy" home and in other areas of the country that same home may sell for $4,000,000.

Yet as you get into the ultra-affluent clientele, they wouldn't have an interest in this type of property as they are generally searching for much more, potentially over $10,000,000.

There is a Difference in Selling a Million Dollar and $40 Million Dollar Property

This simplified example shows you that there is a very specific approach to selling a million dollar property and a very DIFFERENT approach to selling a forty million dollar property.

They are both in the luxury market and they both require wealthy buyers but the marketing campaign must target the specific type of buyer that would have the highest level of interest and also have the financial ability to buy.

Are they affluent or ultra-affluent?

Marketing the home to anyone that is higher or lower than that price range would be an absolute waste of time.

Worse, hiring an agent that spends all of their money to promote their service rather than their houses is even more asinine.

In reality, there is a highly targeted type of buyer that would have the most interest in paying a premium price for a property like yours. But let's look a little deeper.

This is where it gets fun...

The big secret...

Targeting a buyer based on their financial qualifications, net worth, annual household income, etc. is child's play compared to the more advanced approaches.

This is the highly profitable technique that sells property for a lot more money and gets buyers bidding against each other in order to secure the home that they feel is best for their family's needs.

The 'Secret Sauce' To Sell Your Home

It's what I call the "secret sauce" to the superb marketing created by agent members that have been certified as Premier Luxury Marketing Consultants. This could quite possibly be the best way for you to net a great deal more for your property.

Here's how it works. Your property has very distinct amenities that create tremendous value when marketed to the right person. Let me give you a real world example of this for illustration purposes. I think you'll enjoy this story.

Recently, I assisted one of our PLMC Certified agents on a property that was listed for $5,500,000. The property was absolutely gorgeous in the state of Florida right on the Gulf of Mexico. While it had a huge lot and tons of water frontage, one of the best features was a 20 car garage.

Now I want you to think about what type of buyer would have the most interest in a home like this.

As an example, I myself was very impressed by the property when I took a tour of the home. I have the ability and qualifications to buy it and at that time was also looking for a property to purchase.

But there is one little problem. I own 42 racehorses and only 2 cars. As much as I like the house, love the kitchen, would love to go fishing in the Gulf right out back, I'd have absolutely no use for the 20 car garage and it's truly a waste of space.

So instead, I created a tremendous marketing campaign for them. It was incredibly expensive for the agent to market the home with this approach but I want to break it down and show you the math behind this.

It's important for you to know that they were originally listed with another brokerage for over a year with absolutely ZERO offers.

How We Sold a $5.5M Home That Sat For Over A Year In Just 11 Days!

I showed them how I can get a list of people that have a net worth of over $3,000,000 and also have an interest in fishing. I'd do this by merge/purge referencing the list of those with the high net worth with a list of those that subscribe to Florida Fisherman and Saltwater Fishing Magazine.

This list alone would give us a refined group of buyers that have the financial ability to buy and also would have an interest in fishing. Once I had that list, I'd merge/purge against those that have at least 4 cars registered in their name. Now we are getting closer to a perfect match when it comes to a buyer that would fall in love with the property right?

That list was still way too big. So I merge/purged that list with those that also own a boat in the state of Florida, own a home worth between $2,500,000 and $4,000,000 and they've lived there for at least 5 years.

It came back with 1,293 people. When dealing with that particular marketing list broker, I realized that the list

I had to find a list of the most opportune buyers .. they had to have:

1. The correct net worth

2. An interest in fishing

3. More than 4 cars

4. Own a boat in Florida

And I found it!

would be expensive because she is very good at what she does. Due to the extensive "interest selects" that I'd asked for, it required a lot of work on her part and actually became a 6 day project just to gather the data, compile the lists, merge-purge them against each other, remove the duplicates, etc. But I was impressed she got it done.

As it turned out, I'd have to pay $2.77 for each and every one of those contacts with full name, mailing address, email and any available social media or phone information. So the total to acquire that specific list was $3,581.61. Not a bad start at all because we now have a specific list that would have the highest probability of wanting to see the home.

So now I needed to hire a copywriter to create an amazing marketing piece on the property, specifically designed to target this list of prospects utilizing the "interest" categories we discussed here.

I had the ability to separate those that have a fishing

interest from those that have several vehicles in their name so I could have the copywriter create two different marketing pieces to feature each of those criteria.

For those that are qualified financially and show a significant interest in fishing, we'd create a marketing piece they'd be interested in. Meanwhile, those that have the qualifications and have a collection of say 13 cars would get a completely different and totally customized marketing piece.

Once we went through our 2 hour meeting about the property and I showed him some video of the home he got to work with the creation of the marketing piece. It took him

> **I needed to hire a copywriter to create the marketing piece that would ultimately SELL this property.**

4 solid days but came back with an outstanding and compelling offer geared towards the type of buyer that would be most interested in the property.

It ended up being a 9 page sales letter with slight modifications for each interest category and he charged what I believed to be WAY too cheap at a flat fee of $4,600 and no royalty from the results!

An absolute steal compared to what we usually have to

invest for such a thing. If you've ever hired a professional copywriter before, you are probably aware that they are often well over $10,000 plus royalties based on results.

We couldn't have been happier to get such a marketing masterpiece for $4,600.

So now I have an amazing sales letter on a truly spectacular property and I have a list of the absolute most opportune and qualified buyers that may have an interest in purchasing it.

It's starting to get exciting...

I now have to decide how I'm going to get this message out there.

It would be very inexpensive to send the letter to the email address of the contacts I've purchased but there's two problems with that approach. #1 is the list I acquired only had about 70% of the contacts showing a valid email address.

Bad news there.

And #2 is emails will be treated like spam (especially with attachments) so we will get poor results.

We will need to go the direct mail route.

Heck, I can have 1,293 of these printed on good

looking paper in full color for $1.92 each so that's only $2,482.56 in printing.

The issue with direct mail is simply that much of it doesn't get opened because people sort their mail over the trash can.

So I'll need to send this important information in a big Priority Mail envelope. Getting a big cardboard envelope that says "Priority Mail" all over it will get a 100% open rate.

I also want to ensure that I send it on a Thursday because two day priority would be delivered on Saturday.

> **I want my letter to arrive on Saturday – because that is the day that the homeowner is most likely to read and pay attention to it.**

We've found through ample testing that mail delivered on Saturday has a better response rate because people aren't so brutal with their mail as compared to when they get home from work, getting the kids homework done, getting dinner on the oven, letting the dogs out, etc.

To get it delivered on Saturday will drastically increase our rate of people that read the message thoroughly.

We know that we can mail these envelopes to each house for $5.85 in that region so excluding my staff labor cost, I will need to invest $7,564.05 on postage to get this message delivered the right way for maximum results.

As you can imagine, most real estate agents have no idea how to market a property, let alone create such a custom marketing plan targeting the most opportune prospects possible.

The "commodity" type real estate agent would simply send out a postcard saying they listed a house and 50% of the print on that card would be their own face. In my opinion, this is the sole reason so many properties don't sell at all even if they are on the market for a full year.

> **At this point I have invested $18,228.22 to sell this property.**

So I've now invested $3,581.61 to get the specific targeted list, $4,600 for the copywriter, $2,482.56 in printing and postage of $7,564.05. That's a total marketing investment of $18,228.22 plus the labor involved to get it all completed.

I'm sure you'll agree that this investment alone throws out approximately 95% of all real estate agents in town as not only do they have no idea how to do this or where to go to get this type of information, they certainly won't invest significant money into a targeted marketing approach.

Sold in 11 Days
For All Cash!

We had a full price, all cash offer just 11 days later. Better still, the buyers wanted to buy some of the furniture and artwork that was in the home as some of it was custom built for the property. This drove the offer price to $170,000 more than the original asking price.

I should point out that they were listed with another brokerage for over a year before they called one of our Premier Luxury Marketing Consultants.

They never had ONE offer during their original listing.

That's simply because the agent was advertising in random magazines, listing the home on dozens of websites and creating high gloss brochures.

We were able to target the absolute best list.

We marketed to people that had the ability to buy but weren't really actively looking in the market.

This is what we call an OFF-MARKET Buyer.

And since they aren't actively looking at all of the competing homes, we were able to put our home seller into a "category of one" where the buyer looked at only this home, simply because it had all of the features they'd want in a house.

Certainly beats advertising in magazines wouldn't you agree?

So What's The Best Approach To Sell Your Luxury Home?

We do a combination of online and offline marketing and depending on where we can get the best quality list selects, it may be as heavy as 80% to one side or the other.

As an example, one of our luxury marketing approaches involves targeted marketing on-line where we can narrow down people's interests, their income level, homeowners and much more.

Sometimes we market only to CEO's and CFO's with this technique.

This online approach accounts for thousands of home sales every year and it's just one of the many ways we can target them.

Personally, I've found that we've had great success with online and offline approaches but I prefer the offline techniques for several reasons.

Some of it is the privacy of the whole thing (we've sold

homes without the public knowing they are for sale) but generally speaking I prefer it because I have more control over the prospects thoughts and actions if I can get them to sit down in a chair with a specific marketing piece, thus creating better response rates.

> **I think direct mail is the best method because you have more control over who sees your home**

The privacy of the home seller is important and the desired outcome of the seller (an immediate sale at top dollar) goes hand in hand.

This specific marketing approach described (and the investment) is really the secret sauce that sells so many homes for their asking price or higher in a very short window of time. And as you can imagine, it isn't cheap which means you actually GET your desired result.

You'll find that absolutely every certified agent involved with Premier Luxury Marketing Consultants knows this approach inside and out. To find one in your local market, you can go to:

www.PremierLuxuryMarketing.com

CHAPTER 6

Who Will Give You The Highest Price For Your Property?

Several years ago, there used to be a term used in the real estate world which was "highest and best offer".

Essentially, if a seller had a great agent that understood extensive marketing, they'd be able to attract multiple offers and could then ask all of the buyers to submit their "highest and best offer".

In today's world, those are two separate terms. The highest offer may not be the best offer.

Highest Price Doesn't Always Mean Best Offer

Particularly in the luxury market, you'll find that most

of the buyers interested in your property will have a home that they already own so the purchase offers you get may be contingent on the sale of their current property.

Your home is in one of the more affluent price ranges so it won't be sold to a first time home buyer. Since this won't be their first home, they may need to sell their current one in order to get yours.

Keep in mind though, that not everyone would need to sell their home first. They may qualify for a mortgage even though they own another home or better yet, if your house is marketed properly you may get an all cash offer.

Obviously an all cash offer (with proof of funds) is much more desirable than waiting on someone else's home to sell prior to them being able to purchase your property.

In turn, the highest offer may not be the best offer.

One of our certified agents recently represented a homeowner that was selling their home and they were listed at $849,900.

They were able to get two offers, one at full price and the other one just a touch lower at $846,000.

They chose to take the lower offer because it was a better offer with no finance contingencies. It fit into the sellers goals better because it was a "done deal" and could close in 35 to 40 days.

You'll find oftentimes that your highest offer isn't your best offer.

Your agent will be able to help you in deciding which offers will best fit your needs.

More importantly, a properly trained agent will be able to get EVERY offer to a much better position by coming up with alternative ways for the buyer to purchase.

This is generally a few different approaches that the buyer never would have considered otherwise. It may allow them to remove a home sale contingency, close on a property faster or pay more money for the home than they originally thought they could afford. All of these factors are in your best interest as the homeowner.

They'll take average offers and turn them into outstanding offers that are weighted in your best interest.

Finding a Buyer Willing To Pay Top Dollar Is A Function Of <u>YOUR</u> Real Estate Agent

So finding the buyer that will be able to pay the most amount of money may actually come down to the quality of the real estate agent that you have representing you.

There are several steps to consider throughout this

process but the agent needs to be good at identifying the best amenities of your property, finding a specific marketing list based on those interests and selects, understand how to target market those prospects and then negotiate with those prospects knowing why they are so interested in the home in the first place.

All of these factors will determine the overall final sales price. This is where your big win or big loss happens.

To be clear, if you leave this up to a traditional commodity type agent that only focuses on marketing their own services, you may crash and burn with no sale at all.

Worse, it may sell but you'll be in a position that you'd have to accept a lowball offer.

To get the most amount of money for your home it's crucial to choose an agent that knows how to market to the best possible

> **Buyers will ALWAYS try to negotiate UNLESS their desire to acquire is higher than their desire for a 'deal.'**

prospect. Then once we get that big fish on the line, they have to know how to properly reel them in to net you the absolute MOST amount of money possible.

Buyers will always try to negotiate. This is true unless their desire to acquire something is much higher than their internal "greed glands" wanting to get a good deal.

Fear of loss is a major factor in real estate sales and with the unique features your property probably has in the luxury price ranges, it creates a perfect opportunity for an affluent agent to structure the marketing around a tremendous fear of loss if this buyer doesn't take action immediately.

What Are Your Biggest Selling Factors?

As you start this process of selling your home, you'll want to itemize some of the things that you believe are the biggest selling factors.

Upon meeting your PLMC certified real estate agent, they'll ask you for this list so that you can best target a group of buyers that will pay the most amount of money for the home.

Obviously this is a much more proactive approach than you'll generally see which is throwing it on the MLS and waiting on another agent that happens to have a buyer.

Your amenities may consist of a gourmet kitchen, water front property, golf course lot, tennis court, a care takers house, close proximity to an equestrian center, easy access to food and shopping or a large range of other factors.

Every home is unique so you'll want to sincerely think about the amenities so you can provide them to your consultant.

This will be the "bait" they'll be able to use in attracting the big fish so be sure that you get them all together prior to the initial meeting.

They'll be able to utilize that list to come up with the best "selects" when creating a direct marketing campaign.

By creating this list and trying to get a PLMC certified agent to accept the project, you are doing everything within your power to net the highest possible price for your property.

As you can see, this creates a highly customized approach that sheds your home in the best light to the best prospects and puts your best foot forward.

CHAPTER 7

Should Your Home Sale Be Public or Private?

This is a very common question asked by affluent homeowners all over the United States.

Most people that are wealthy or towards the "upper end" as far as finances go usually try to be very private with their business dealings.

Understandable of course.

This oftentimes includes their home sale.

It may surprise you to know that up to 30% of the homeowners we meet with in their home initially start out believing they'd like to have a private sale with no sign in the yard, no MLS, no public ads or newspapers, etc.

Once they weigh their options, they generally change their mind but fortunately with a solid marketing campaign, either way is fine. Let's look at both sides here for just a moment.

Sign or No Sign?

Privacy in a sale makes a homeowner feel at ease because they don't have to worry about what the neighbors see regarding the sale, the price, etc.

They also have a perception that it is "safer" to not be a public sale. It's very common for an affluent homeowner to be against any type of virtual tour or streaming movie of the home for security reasons.

This is especially true if they have a large amount of valuable artwork or expensive décor that could be seen on any of those streaming videos.

An owner of a high end home may consider a private sale for this as well as a number of other reasons.

Most owners realize that putting the home on the Multiple Listing Service makes it "public".

All of the real estate agents in town will know it's for sale, the property listing gets syndicated on various other websites and it is searchable by anyone looking to purchase a home.

The Highest Exposure...

This is certainly a good thing for the exposure it needs but you have to be sincerely wanting to sell to go this route.

We don't have to worry about what the neighbors think (since they won't be neighbors for long) and we have to be okay with everyone being able to search and see that the home is on the open market.

This would include the asking price, requested terms and more.

Not having a sign out front will generally eliminate any issues of neighbors knowing about the home being for sale anyway, even if it is listed on the open market.

Obviously they aren't looking on various websites or contacting their agent every week to ask them if your home is on the market.

If there's no sign and no ads in the local paper, they'll likely never even know it is for sale.

You can still get a customized and elaborate marketing plan yet the general public (neighbors, co-workers, ex-spouses, etc.) wouldn't see anything unless they are actively looking to purchase a home.

With all of this in mind, it's important to remember

that your family's primary goal is to get this property sold so that you can move on to your next house.

Delaying the process or eliminating your chance at buyers by trying to keep things "secret" may cost you more money than it's actually worth.

It's very possible for a Premier Luxury Marketing Consultant to sell your property without the MLS but you'll want to weigh your options and decide if that's a route you want to consider.

They'll tell you the positives and the negatives to both options but from years and years of experience, I'll tell you that it's always better have the property listed in the MLS.

Listing In The MLS

You'll always sell your home faster and for more money with a direct marketing approach.

Your PLMC agent can show you some of the best selects to create that buyer frenzy but you'll also want to be publicly listed so that they can utilize their Buyer Agent Network throughout the region to work with the other real estate agents that may have a buyer.

Oftentimes due to the agent's extensive marketing campaigns, they may want to keep the home sale private for 2 to 4 weeks.

If they haven't sold the home by then, they'll have the public listing exposure begin. In most cases, it's best to voice your interests, goals and concerns with your agent and then let them lead you in the right direction so that you'll end up with your desired outcome.

Remember, they are professionals at this so if you are honest and upfront with what you want as well as any concerns you may have, you'll be able to work as a team in getting to those desired goals.

Ultimately, you have to decide upon your motivation and sincerity in getting your home sold before you make the decision on being public or private.

A public sale will always get you a bit more exposure so I'd recommend you go that route. However, every situation is different and you'll want to discuss your thoughts with your Premier Luxury Marketing Consultant.

The one caution I will throw your way is to avoid making decisions on this topic based on ego or worrying about what other people may think.

You have to do what's best for you and your family and you can make decisions on something this important based on what a neighbor or friend may think.

Get the thing sold, net as much as you possibly can by

making good choices in representation and the rest just
falls into place.

CHAPTER 8

Avoiding the "Commodity Type" Real Estate Agent

One of the biggest mistakes a homeowner can make in the luxury real estate market is hiring the wrong agent to sell their home.

It can create an absolute disaster.

Most homeowners love their home so they mistakenly believe that it's going to sell regardless of who represents them.

While sometimes this is the case, not only may it take a long time for that to happen, but it may also be at a final sale price MUCH lower than you originally thought you'd receive.

Remember, selling and selling at the right price are two completely different things.

And "demanding" a high price or telling them you won't sell is the same as deciding not to sell at all in the first place.

Regardless of your motivation to liquidate this asset, you can't muscle your way into a strong offer from a bunch of weak buyers.

Ultimately, you'd end up staying in your home so don't set yourself up for this type of disappointment by utilizing a "below par" marketing specialist.

How Do You Choose A Real Estate Agent To Sell Your Home?

Unfortunately, uneducated homeowners think it makes sense to hire an agent that they've heard of in the past or whom they believe to be "famous" because they see their photo advertised everywhere.

After all, in lieu of all measurements, that makes sense right? If you've heard of them, there's a good chance everyone else has too maybe?

Even worse is the owner that believes they should list their property with the agent that helped them to buy the property when they first acquired it.

While you certainly know this agent personally and they were the one that drove you around to look at homes, it gives them zero qualifications for aggressively marketing the home with a professional direct marketing campaign.

A buyer's agent and a listing agent are two completely different things and in a category far above both of them is a Premier Luxury Marketing Consultant.

You now have in your hands a better measurement of success and specific instructions on how you can use someone that will utilize a target marketing approach on your home.

This will use a highly specific game plan to find the most opportune buyer and sell that buyer on the specific features and amenities that will most excite them.

What is A "Commodity Type" Real Estate Agent?

To avoid the "commodity type" agent, you have to first know what it is.

I'm sure you are aware that the typical job called "real estate agent" has been commoditized.

Putting it in the MLS, fielding the phone calls, showing the home, writing the contract and handling the closing can be done by anyone.

And frankly speaking, in most areas it can be done for $99.00. As you can imagine, you get what you pay for and from the research I've repeatedly seen, these are oftentimes the homes that don't sell at all or worse, sell for hundreds of thousands of dollars under their original asking price.

These homeowners thought they were saving money by getting a "discount" on their commission but in reality, they created a discount in their marketing exposure and representation so they sold for far less than they ever imagined they would.

This is especially true in the luxury market. After all, you've seen plenty of times in life what happens when you take a "cheap" option.

I'm sure you can think of countless times you went with a "cheap" option and got just that. It generally costs you more in the long run to repair that mess and this is especially true in the sale of real estate.

A superior real estate agent will invest thousands of dollars in marketing to ensure that your home sells for the most amount of money possible.

THIS is how you net a higher price at the closing table. By choosing an agent based on the commission that they charge, you may be cutting off your own nose.

There's no way an agent can invest a tremendous amount of money in marketing if there's not much commission at the end of the rainbow.

This causes them to cut corners, eliminate expenses and simply "hope" that the home sells.

All of this creates a bad situation for you and there's simply no way to win by dealing with an agent that's cut their own commission.

Finding the BEST Buyer Isn't Cheap

We've already discussed where the BEST buyers come from and while an extremely well trained marketing professional can find them fairly easily, it's certainly not cheap.

Those buyers that may be willing to pay you an additional $50,000 or $100,000 for your home can be acquired and attracted but it will be at an investment of lots of marketing dollars and research.

Since most of the affluent home buyers we've surveyed said that they were not in the market to buy when they found out about the home they recently purchased, it stands to reason that an agent is wasting their time by advertising in the magazines, websites and other advertising media that the active buyer is looking in.

The better approach is to find out who is most likely to fall in love with the specific amenities and benefits offered with your home, cross reference it with those that can afford the purchase, and target market specifically to them.

It doesn't matter if they are actively in the market or not. You'll find that when wealthy citizens of America want something bad enough, they'll get it.

This is true even if they weren't necessarily shopping for it in the first place.

As an example, in an earlier chapter I discussed the fact that I own over 3 dozen racehorses.

This includes not only those that we are racing, but also those that we breed and raise. So even though I am not actively in the market today to buy a property and I have no idea what is available on the market near the area that my horse trainers work, I'll assure you that if someone contacted me with the perfect property, I'd be buying.

Let's say for instance that this property is on 40 acres, it has a 50 stall barn with superior ventilation, there are fences all around the property, it has a separate living quarters for the caretakers and grooms and there's a small exercise track as well.

I'm interested and I'll assure you I'd take a look at it. As a matter of fact, I'd take a private jet there to see the property.

Oh, I almost forgot, does it have a house on the property? It doesn't really matter to me either way. For those interested in amenities like this, the house is an afterthought.

> **If it's the right property for me ... I'd take a private jet today to look at it. And I am not actively looking for properties.**

Frankly, I'm the type of person that would probably tear it down and rebuild a masterpiece anyway. If it fits my needs for the things that I'm passionate about, the house on the property is the least of my concerns.

I'm sure you've seen two million to ten million dollar homes torn down to completely rebuild so that the buyer will have something they'd like to live in. When you get into the luxury market, these issues are trivial.

As you can imagine, this direct marketing approach is a much better option than trying to sell this very unique home to someone that is actively in the market, looking on the MLS, shopping around at various properties and weighing each of them against each other.

Think about your own property for a moment. It

certainly has several unique features. Imagine it's in close proximity to something desirable or would be perfect for a home based business or something that's close to the airport for the traveling CEO.

These are all factors that we should accentuate in our marketing to net more money from the sale of the property.

We Have To Be IN FRONT Of The Best Buyers

We have to get it in front of the best type of buyer that would have an immediate desire to learn more about it. This won't happen just from throwing the home up on the open market.

You need a Premier Luxury Marketing Consultant to put this together for you properly and to ensure that the buyers that come along would do anything to secure the home for their own needs.

You can get more info on this and find local PLMC Certified representatives for your area at: **www.PremierLuxuryMarketing.com**

I'll give you a sincere word of caution here regarding your upcoming home sale.

I've personally met, coached and spoken from the stage

to over 30,000 real estate agents around the country. So I certainly understand what happens "behind the curtain" in real estate sales.

In my professional experience I can tell you that nothing is more dangerous than hiring a real estate agent that doesn't have the true credentials required to create a target marketing approach for your home.

Less than 1% of all agents in America are certified as a Premier Luxury Marketing Consultant.

If you have one in your area, I would encourage you to do everything within your power to get them to accept your project and

> **It's more dangerous to hire an agent who doesn't truly know how to MARKET luxury properties**

invest their own money into an extensive marketing campaign.

They won't accept all of the projects that are presented to them, but if they feel like it may be a good fit and they are confident they'll be able to reach your goals, you'll be able to secure them for your luxury property sale.

Greg Luther, Founder of Premier Luxury Marketing Consultants

CHAPTER 9

How To Find A Premier Luxury Marketing Consultant

At the last total I've seen, there are over 1,000,000 real estate agents in the United States. And the average agent earns less than $40,000 per year. This is a stat provided by the National Association of Realtors®.

Many would say this is a humiliating stat and it's certainly not something they'd want to depend on for the sale of your home.

When you are looking for a real estate agent that will invest a large sum of money to target market your home (rather than marketing their own face) you'll need to ensure they have the knowledge, access and ability to put a tremendous campaign in place.

An average agent would have no idea how to do this with a luxury property.

Needless to say they probably won't have the access, knowledge or ability to do it either.

This is one of the reasons I created Premier Luxury Marketing Consultants and the PLMC designation.

I've coached and mentored over 30,000 real estate agents and owned brokerages all over the country. Let me tell you the facts.

Most Real Estate agents invest less than $1,000 into marketing an individual property

Most real estate agents never invest even $1,000 into their marketing of an individual listing, thus the reason that nearly half of all luxury homes we researched never sold at all during their initial listing agreement.

Half The Properties NEVER Sold...

That's right, in our study we found that over half of them didn't sell at all.

This is the same properties where the owner met with an agent, had supreme confidence that their home would sell and just knew they'd get their price very quickly.

Fast forwarding to the end of their agreement, they reduced their original price and we found that it was still a miserable failure. This is an absolute lose/lose situation. Remember one thing...

They Can't Buy Your Home If They Don't Know It's For Sale!

Exposing your property to the right people is truly the key to success in a happy and profitable home sale. And this can be assured when utilizing an agent that's been through the rigorous training and testing required for the PLMC designation.

Keep in mind that the only way any agent in the country can gain access to this training and designation is to specifically seek me out and invest a very large sum of time, money and focus to learn how to correctly market a luxury property like yours.

Once they learn the details on specific approaches to utilizing target marketing, list selects and an extensive campaign, they have the ability to create the best exposure for YOUR property.

There's no better way for an agent to learn these techniques than to learn from other highly productive luxury agents residing all over the country.

We teach them through case studies, marketing examples and real world hands-on training prior to them earning their certification.

To be clear with you, this is not some NAR endorsed course designed by boards and committees to get as much money as possible from their members.

It's not created, promoted or provided by them in any way. This is designed by and designed specifically for the multi-million dollar agents that want to absolutely dominate the luxury housing market with superior service, superior marketing and superior results.

This creates a win/win for the agents as well as the buyers and sellers they represent in the luxury market.

Many of the agents that have become certified as a PLMC real estate agent have become incredibly busy in their local markets so they are sometimes hard to secure an appointment with but they are well worth the time from an educational perspective just to see the difference in what they can do for you to increase the exposure and quite possibly the sales price of your home.

If you are reading this book and you've gotten this far, there's a good chance that the book was referred to you by one of our PLMC Certified agents.

This is the person for you to contact regarding the sale of your home. As we've discussed thus far, they are exceptionally qualified to expose your home to the absolutely best, most opportune buyers that would be willing to pay at or above full market price.

It's Your Number One Job...

In my personal experience, I've found that the number one job of a homeowner when considering a sale is <u>to choose the BEST agent</u> to <u>net them the absolute most amount of money</u> from the sale of their home.

The big mistakes are choosing an agent that has essentially made themselves famous by marketing their face instead of their homes or choosing an agent based on the fee they charge, regardless of what you actually get for that fee.

For many homeowners, even in the luxury price ranges, their home is usually one of their top 3 assets they own from an equity standpoint.

In turn, it should be treated as such. There's a good chance that when you are considering a large stock purchase you don't use the $7.00 discount broker. You probably go with a very reputable broker that can give you advice on what to do, what not to do and some of the pitfalls to avoid.

You Wouldn't Buy Stocks From A Discount Broker – Why Would You Do So For Your Home?

It's very helpful to get the perspective from a qualified third party, rather than someone trying to earn a cheap fee.

That cheap fee can cost you a fortune right?

The same is true with your home sale.

You wouldn't trust an investment like this to someone that's unqualified. And it's an absolute ridiculous decision to go with the agent that quotes you an asking price higher than anyone else does.

If that's your goal, keep shopping around. You are sure to find an agent that would be willing to list the home at two million dollars more than anyone else. My advice has always been that if you are going to do that, just shoot for an even ten million dollars more because the sale has exactly a ZERO percent chance of happening anyway.

Truth be told, the empirical evidence of home value is just that, it's the evidence you should use for pricing decisions.

The Evidence To Justify
Your Home's Value...

The homes that have sold in your general area are not an opinion of price, but they are the actual evidence used to justify your home's value to the bank or investor.

You can stretch towards the top level of that range but you have to remember that even if you get a buyer to agree to a certain price, you still have to get it to appraise.

And the shady appraisers are all in prison now. So the pricing of the home comes AFTER you've chosen the absolute best real estate agent to sell the home for the most amount of money by providing a targeted marketing campaign.

Greg Luther, Founder of Premier Luxury Marketing Consultants

CHAPTER 10

What To Do First

Before you decide to actually list your home for sale and officially make the move, it's wise to take the best approach in ensuring you play your cards right from the very beginning.

The last thing you'd want to do is "pull the trigger" before you are truly prepared to do so.

In this short chapter, I'll distill the knowledge acquired from being involved with the inner workings of thousands of luxury home sales all over the country.

I've worked with these homeowners on my own account, or in conjunction with all of our Premier Luxury Marketing Consultants from sea to shining sea.

What Are You
Trying To Sell?

In making the right move for yourself, you need to first consider what it is that you are trying to sell.

You are selling much more than a house. It's also more than a luxury priced house. You are actually selling location, amenities, specific usage, peace of mind, an outstanding trophy and many other criteria that the right buyer would be willing to pay a premium for.

> **The first thing you need to do is decide what great features your home has to offer**

The first thing you need to do is sit down and decide on all of the great features your property has to offer.

I've given a few examples in the previous chapters. After documenting this list, you can provide it for your real estate agent and their marketing team to ensure they are target marketing to the absolute best potential buyers.

As the property owner, you may be thinking about interviewing one or two other agents while also interviewing a local Premier Luxury Marketing Consultant real estate agent.

It's wise to show them the list of these features and

amenities and ask them how they'd best use them for the benefit of the sale.

What You Should Ask Your Real Estate Agent

This will be a great exercise to ensure you are securing a marketing specialist that knows how to properly expose the home in its best light.

In my totally biased and professional opinion, I think it's crucial for you to choose an agent that is certified as a Premier Luxury Marketing Consultant.

These are the agents that specialize in high end properties just like yours and they know how to maximize the equity position for affluent homeowners in their local marketplace.

They've invested a great deal of time, money and focus on structuring their business model to sell high level homes at a significant premium.

It's wise to contact the agent that shared this information with you. We have Luxury Home Consultants all over the country but you'll want to utilize one that is in your local marketplace and expresses an interest in working with a property like yours.

Before I get your hopes up too high here, I should

make a damaging admission to you.

If you've ever worked with typical real estate agents in the past, you are probably aware that most of them will say whatever they need to say to get the listing.

You'll quickly find that this isn't the case with PLMC Certified Agents. As a matter of fact, they generally turn down more projects than they accept.

The Type of Real Estate Agent You Want...

You have to remember that with an extensive marketing plan like this, the agent will be investing several thousand dollars of their own money so if they don't think they can meet your needs, they'd rather turn you down now than to let you down later.

They wouldn't be willing to invest a great deal of their own money if they don't believe they can logically get it to the closing table.

The typical agent that isn't investing much would have no problem at all signing up a listing even if they know there's barely a slight chance they'd have success in selling.

After all, what do they have to lose?

This is not a relationship you want to enter when it

comes to the sale of your property.

The goal of your move is to make it as seamless and smooth as possible while still selling for the absolute most amount of net profit.

In turn, you want to get out of the commodity approach and go with a high quality premium representative.

Then let the results speak for themselves.

If you do set up a meeting with a local PLMC certified real estate agent, they'll gladly meet with you with no obligation on your part or theirs.

They will offer a "Fast-Start" consultation which will give you tips on what to do and what not to do in preparing the home for sale.

Additionally, they'll be able to point out the key factors of your home that could be exploited for a higher sales price and may even discuss their proprietary approach to marketing the home to the most opportune buyer.

You can have this meeting with a local professional just to get a better handle on timing, how to best structure your offer and much more.

And once you get this information, you can then decide

if it's best to sell the home now or further prepare for a sale at a later date.

Again, do a little bit of research at **www.PremierLuxuryMarketing.com** and chat with a local PLMC certified agent.

You'll see a difference that's absolutely "night and day" compared to the run-of-the-mill traditional approach. This educational meeting will help you to shed a little bit of light on your best approach, will help you to decide on your game plan and timing and ultimately will make you feel more confident and prepared for a sale whenever that time is right.

My hope is that this brief book was helpful in assisting you to consider some better options in selling your home for top dollar.

Since I've worked with so many luxury level sellers in different capacities, I certainly understand how important it is to sell for as much as possible.

More importantly, I know what it takes to sell for top dollar. It's not cheap, but it can allow you to net more than anyone would customarily realize with a traditional approach.

I'd recommend that you get with a local PLMC

Certified agent immediately.

Have a quick meeting, get their information and get some ideas on how they can expose your property to a better quality group of buyers.

I think you'd find it to be incredibly valuable and most importantly, can allow your transition to happen smoothly with the most amount of profit possible.

Go to **www.PremierLuxuryMarketing.com** and learn how you can sell your property for more than you ever thought possible.

ABOUT THE AUTHOR

Greg Luther was born and raised in Columbus, Ohio. He entered the real estate field with the dreams of helping those in his community find their ideal homes. But he struggled, as so many agents do. He knew there had to be a better way – and after years of studying successful people (not just real estate agents) he figured out through target - marketing his properties, he was finally able to bring ideal buyers and seller together and secure the highest value for the homes.

It wasn't long before he had agents banging down the door to learn these secrets and over the last 10 years he has shared his secrets with over 30,000 agents.

He founded Premier Luxury Marketing Consultants to provide home sellers with one place they could go to find highly qualified Real Estate Agents, each extensively trained in his marketing approach to attract ideal buyers, happily willing to pay top dollar and close on your home quickly. All of these agents specialize in the luxury market within their town and have demonstrated significant investment in learning how to sell their properties for more money.

Greg can be reached by fax only at 614-573-7150.

Made in the USA
Las Vegas, NV
03 June 2021